Three Simple Rules

for Christian Living

Jeanne Torrence Finley

ABINGDON PRESS
NASHVILLE

THREE SIMPLE RULES FOR CHRISTIAN LIVING

ISBN 978-1-426-70025-5

09 10 11 12 13 14 15 16 17—10 9 8 7 6 5 4

MANUFACTURED IN THE UNITED STATES OF AMERICA

CONTENTS

Introduction

Since it was published in 2007, Bishop Rueben Job's *Three Simple Rules* has been widely read and studied. Extended reflection on the three rules can lead us to a more faithful way of living as disciples of Christ. This study, *Three Simple Rules for Christian Living*, is an effort to provide such extended reflection.

John Wesley believed that following Christ in a way that renews both individuals and communities required disciplined practices. These were outlined in the "General Rules" that Wesley wrote for the class meetings that were the core communities of the early Methodist movement. These disciplined practices gave power and strength to people of the early Methodist movement to live as faithful disciples of Jesus Christ.

Bishop Job, in lifting up these "three simple rules," helps us return to those early Wesleyan roots and find resources that can transform us and the world in which we live. Job calls us to consider these three rules as an alternative to the often frenzied, divisive, and destructive lifestyle our culture offers us. This alternative way of life is accessible to everyone regardless of age, financial standing, education, health, relative power, or theological understandings.

Our culture has forgotten the importance of community and stressed ndividualism too much. Often we in the church have not taken the gospel seriously but have focused on trivialities and divisions that distract us from loving God and neighbor. We drain our witness to God's redemptive power as we find ever new ways to harm each other. Bishop Job calls us to remember who we are: people who know about practices of forgiveness, reconciliation, transformation, and new life.

Job calls these three rules "a way of holy living that is constantly reforming and renewing the individual and the community" (*Three Simple Rules*; p. 17). They are Christian practices that also heal the wounds of the world and work for justice. Loving God results in loving the world. Job writes, "Spiritual disciplines not only include practices that bind us to God every day; but they also include actions that heal the pain, injustice, and inequality of our world. It is impossible to stay in love with God and not desire to see God's goodness and grace shared with the entire world" (*Three Simple Rules*; p. 58).

As you read and reflect on these rules, you'll notice that they are interrelated. The first two rules, "do no harm" and "do good," are ways of keeping the commandments to love God and neighbor. When we explore rule three, "stay in love with God," we'll see that the particular disciplines that keep us in close relationship to God are practices through which God empowers us to love God and neighbor.

In these pages we will be reflecting on what these rules meant to Wesley and the early Methodist movement and what they can mean to us today. Then we will explore ways we can practice them in our own lives. I invite you to take this journey of exploration and reflection so as to discover ever deepening ways you can be formed and renewed in the Christian life.

—Jeanne Torrence Finley

Jeanne Torrence Finley is a clergy member of the Virginia Conference of the United Methodist Church, co-chair of the Virginia Conference Board of Church and Society, and director of Collegial Communications. She has worked as a campus minister, pastor, college English teacher, workshop leader, and communications consultant. Finley writes regularly for *FaithLink*. Her work has appeared in the *Journal of Presbyterian History, Worship, The Mennonite, Christian Science Monitor*, the *Virginia Advocate*, and *Christian Social Action*.

Chapter 1

Do No Harm –
Understanding the Rule

Focus Question:

Most Christians do not intend to harm anyone; however, we sometimes are not aware of the harm we do. What does it mean to "do no harm"?

A Prayer

God of love, we know you want us to love your creation: neighbors, friends or enemies, strangers, the natural world, and ourselves. Yet we do harm, often unintentionally. Help us to be more aware of the harm we do. In Christ we pray. Amen.

WHAT DOES THE RULE SAY?

Unintended Harm

When we moved into our current house, we realized our basement stairs weren't build to present-day code. Most of the treads were shorter than the average adult foot; and in the turn of the stairway, the treads were even shorter. In addition, the risers weren't built in correct proportion to the treads; and halfway down, anyone over six feet tall had to duck to avoid the ceiling. When we had guests, I'd put a sign on the door that said, "Beware! Weird stairs!"

A look through a daily newspaper will reveal all kinds of unintended harm. A driver hasn't kept her car in good repair, the brakes fail, and a pedestrian is injured. A distracted nurse gives a patient medicine intended for another, and the patient's condition worsens. A pet owner tells the neighbors that his dog won't bite, but the dog attacks a child.

The first rule, "do no harm," is easy enough to understand; but following it can be challenging. The builder of the weird stairs didn't intend to hurt anyone, but the potential for harm was there. The driver, the nurse, and the dog owner didn't intend harm; but people were hurt. Most of us most of the time don't intend to harm anyone, but we are often unaware of the harm we do. What does it mean to do no harm?

Reflect on the Rule

How Aware Are You? Assess your awareness of what it means to do harm by writing responses to the following questions.

Where is harm being done? (Use an example from your household or circle of friends, your family, your congregation, your community, your city, your state, a group of people with whom you identify, your nation, or the world.)

Who is being harmed?

What harm is being done?

Who is doing it or causing it? (The "who" may be one or more people, groups, corporations, institutions, states, or nations.)

Why is it happening?

How is harm being done?

Rueben Job in *Three Simple Rules* tells us that these rules are simple but not easy. This first rule may seem the hardest of the three to follow; but it has clear benefits, not only to those we might harm but to ourselves. Job declares that in the middle of difficult situations "it often saved me from uttering a wrong word or considering a wrong response." This rule "can provide a safe place to stand while the hard and faithful work of discernment is done" (*Three Simple Rules*; p. 21). Job recommends this rule to groups engaged in conflict. Agreeing to this rule can change the climate of the conflict, keeping us from gossip, manipulation, and injury to the character of opponents. Following this rule can help us see our commonalities, reduce our fear of the other, and bring forth creativity and insight. However, following this rule can be quite challenging. It demands self-discipline and faith that God will lead us; and as Job writes, it demands "a *radical trust* in God's presence, power, wisdom, and guidance and a *radical obedience* to God's leadership" (p. 24). The rule makes further demands on us. It may take us places we'd rather not go, cause us to relinquish our power, and require us to entertain the thought that we may be wrong. Job assures us, "The good news is that we don't have to make this journey alone. There is *always* One who stands there with us" (p. 28).

How do you respond to Job's understanding that the rule "do no harm" can provide a safe place to stand during the work of discernment? Why do you think the rule requires radical trust and obedience in God?

John Wesley's General Rules

When Wesley composed the General Rules for the societies, bands, and classes of the early Methodist movement, he listed some examples of harm to avoid.[1] Job describes them as sounding "quaint and dated" to our ears (*Three Simple Rules*; p. 17). Twenty-first-century Christians may be surprised at how many of these ways of doing harm have an economic dimension—working on Sunday, buying and selling on Sunday, slaveholding, not paying sales taxes, participating in usury (lending money at unlawful or exorbitant rates), wearing expensive clothing or jewelry, buying or selling distilled alcohol. Some of these are about harm done to our relationship with God and with other people, and some are about both.

Wesley's list represents what he saw, and much of it was about harm to the poor. Using sources of knowledge available to him in the 18th century, Wesley looked for the root causes of poverty and saw that the shift from an agrarian economy to an industrial one was part of the problem. Britain had fenced off common land. Small farmers were getting poorer while the wealthy were getting richer from agriculture. Unskilled workers left the countryside in search of jobs in the city, sometimes to no avail. Households in the country suffered from lack of income while the increased number of unskilled workers in cities drove down wages. Some of these ways of doing harm were related to the indulgences and luxuries of the rich. Spending money on unnecessary items was a stewardship issue. Resources that could have helped the poor were often wasted by those who had money. The use of distilled alcohol and the number of horses owned by the wealthy were driving up the price of grain. Wesley saw these factors as robbing the poor.[2]

> If you were writing John Wesley's General Rules for doing no harm today, what would you put on the list?
>
> **Reflect**

The Answers Depend on the Questions

When we look at John Wesley's rule to do no harm, we may ask: what harm am I doing? We examine ourselves for ways we might hurt other people—gossiping, taking revenge on our enemies, undercutting a co-worker's efforts, starting rumors about people we don't like, or making someone else look bad. Of course, it is important to discipline ourselves to avoid doing harm; but we can also prevent harm by looking at the bigger picture. Instead of asking only "What harm am I doing?" we could begin with a more comprehensive set of questions. Who or what is being harmed? What harm is being done to them? Who, collectively, is doing it? Am I one of them? If so, what can I do to stop the harm?

> How do the questions in this paragraph affect your awareness of harm caused by groups or institutions? How might you unwittingly be part of the group?
>
> **Reflect**

Of course, these questions work on the individual level. We may note that we are harming ourselves by not taking care of our health or not being good stewards of our resources. We may be harming our neighbors and co-workers by gossip and character defamation. We may be harming our families by neglect or poor communication. Once we identify the harm we do, we are empowered to be more vigilant not to do it.

If John Wesley were living in the 21st century, I believe he would be reading widely, seeking to understand not only religion but also economics, sociology, globalization, science, medicine, international relations, arts, and literature. He would constantly be looking for connections among all these subjects in order to make sense of culture and the human condition, especially human suffering. He would want to know where harm is being done and what he and "the people called Methodists" could be doing to stop it.

Wesley believed Christian discipleship was chiefly a matter of loving God and neighbor, a matter that could not be separated from seeing where and how the neighbor was being harmed. In Wesley's view, God is "the Proprietor" of creation and we human beings are stewards.[3] Our bodies, our capacity to work, and indeed the created order belong to God; and God entrusted them to us. We may have used our energies and skills to buy property, but the property and the profit that comes from it belong to God. We are accountable to God for everything that is entrusted to us—talent, time, resources of nature, skills, and the tools of our trade.[4]

A student once complained to me that she didn't like the written prayers in Sunday worship services. After all, they weren't about her. She didn't like the idea of confessing something that she didn't do. No one had ever taught her that the prayers of worship are the prayers of the Christian community or that the Lord's Prayer begins with "Our Father," not with "My Father," and that in it "we" pray for "our daily bread" and "we" ask that "our trespasses" be forgiven. We may have grown up in families or churches where sin was entirely individual. We were taught that as individuals we should not steal or lie or covet, but hardly anyone ever mentioned the sin of collections of people—corporations, institutions, and other groupings. That's why the questions about harm need to begin in a more comprehensive way that helps us to see the harm.

When we open our eyes to the harm done, we see much—the hungry, the exploited, the jobless, the people who work for much less than a living wage, the children who lack health care, the sexually abused, the forgotten, the lost, the last, and the least. We see environmental harm— endangered species, careless use of nonrenewable resources, pollution, and global warming. And then when we ask who is doing this, if not directly, at least indirectly, we also need to ask: Are we in any way a part of that collective group; and if so, how can we stop the harm? Are we invested, either monetarily or emotionally, in efforts that cause harm? These are hard questions to ask, but if we don't ask them, we are missing the point of Christian discipleship.

If you see yourself as part of the group or institution that might be causing harm, what changes could you make? How might you influence change in the group or institution to make changes that would reduce the harm being done?

Reflect

WHAT DOES THE BIBLE SAY?

Do you remember preparing to get your driver's license? Maybe you had a little book to study to learn the rules of the road. Maybe you took a driving class in school. Either way, you learned a number of basic rules. When you first sat down behind the wheel of a car, you had to think about those rules; but after you gained some experience, they became "second nature" to you. Now you probably don't think about them much at all and if asked about their reason for being, you might look at the questioner in disbelief and say, "What do you think? They keep us from hurting and killing each other."

Read Exodus 20:1-17. What connections do you see between the Ten Commandments and the rule to do no harm?

Reflect on the Bible

Many of us learned the Ten Commandments years before we ever learned the rules for driving. Some of them we would never intentionally break—do not kill and do not steal. Others we break when it seems harmless to do so—remember the sabbath and do not covet, for example. One seems not to apply to us at all—do not make an idol. Most of us give little thought to the ethical principles behind them.

Why did the Israelites and their religious descendents, which include us, need the Ten Commandments? The simple answer is to keep us from hurting and killing each other. Although there are more complex answers than this one, answers explaining the history and self-understandings of the Hebrew people and their relationship to God, in this brief space, we'll consider a highly condensed answer. God, the Creator and Lover of creation, wants us to live in love, wholeness, and freedom. The specific example of God's love in the Exodus story is that God has delivered the people Israel from slavery in Egypt and has made covenant with them. The boundaries that protect and empower the Hebrew people, who were chosen to serve God and carry out God's dream for the beloved creation, are expressed in the Ten Commandments.

> **Reflect**
>
> Which of the commandments concern doing no harm? In each, what kind of harm is prohibited? Who is being protected from harm? Do any of these commandments also protect the one who might do harm? If so, how?

Ultimate Loyalty

Central to understanding all of the Ten Commandments are the first two—which paradoxically seem to be the ones that do not directly say "do no harm." The first one, with preface, is key to all the others: "I am the LORD your God, who brought you out the land of Egypt, out of the house of slavery; you shall have no other gods before me" (Exodus 20:2-3). This is the declaration that God has acted out of love to give life and freedom to God's people. Their ultimate loyalty is to God alone. If they give their ultimate loyalty to someone or something else, they will do harm—to themselves and to others. The second commandment against idolatry flows from the first and basically reiterates it. We are to worship God and God alone, not things, not other people, not institutions, not governments, not our own power, and not our talents and ambitions. In other words, God comes first. Although in our time, we don't routinely see statues of gods in our towns, we do have the tendency to make gods of many things. The things we value most may function as our "gods." Sometimes it's been said that if we follow the first two commandments we're not as likely to break the other ones.

If our highest loyalty is to God, then we will love what God loves, and that is the foundation of living so as to do no harm.

> What are your ultimate loyalties? What might your checkbook or credit card statement tell you about what you value most? To what goals do you give your greatest efforts? What does your lifestyle tell you and other people about your values? Are your ultimate loyalties doing harm to what God loves: the earth and all of creation, including human creatures?

Reflect

CLOSING—A GUIDE FOR DAILY PRAYER

Welcoming God's Presence

Gracious God, open our eyes to love what you love so that we will do no harm.

Uphold and guide us during this season of Lent as we seek to follow your commandments and abide in your ways. Amen.

Scripture

"The law of the LORD is perfect,
    reviving the soul;
the decrees of the LORD are sure,
    making wise the simple;
the precepts of the LORD are right,
    rejoicing the heart; . . .
But who can detect their errors?
    Clear me from hidden faults.
Keep back your servant also from the insolent;
    do not let them have dominion over me."
                        — Psalm 19:7-8, 12-13a

Meditation

Reflect on Psalm 19:7-8, 12-13a in terms of the admonition to do no harm. Write down your insights from this reflection:

Conclude with
"Let the words of my mouth and the meditation of my heart
    be acceptable in your sight,
    O LORD, my rock and my redeemer."
                — Psalm 19:14

Prayer

Pray for seeing the potential for harm and for forgiveness for harm done. Intercede for those who have suffered harm, and pray for strength and wisdom to do no harm.

Blessing

"In returning and rest you shall be saved;
in quietness and in trust shall be your strength."
                — Isaiah 30:15b

---

[1] See this list in "The Nature, Design, and General Rules of Our United Societies," ¶ 103 in *The Book of Discipline of The United Methodist Church* (The United Methodist Publishing House, 2004); p. 73.

[2] Sondra Wheeler, "John Wesley and 'Social Ethics,' " From the website of The Project on Lived Theology at the University of Virginia; www.livedtheology.org/pdfs.

[3] John Wesley, Sermon 87, "The Danger of Riches," (text from the 1872 edition – Thomas Jackson, ed.). From website of The United Methodist Church; http://new.gbgm-umc.org/umhistory/wesley/sermons/.

[4] Sondra Wheeler, "Wielding the Sword: John Wesley's Biblical Hermeneutics on Wealth"; http://www.oxford-institute.org/meetings/2007/grouppapers.html.

Chapter

Do No Harm –
Practicing the Rule

Focus Question:

How can we put into practice the rule of doing no harm? What difference can our practice make in our own lives and in the lives of others?

A Prayer

God of love and grace, when our anger, indignation, indifference, or greed cause us to want to do harm, give us strength and courage to resist. When we think you are asking the impossible of us, give us the mindfulness and strength to do no harm. Amen.

WHAT DOES THE RULE SAY?

What Would You Never Do?

My daughter Anne recently had a phone interview for a teaching position in another state from where she presently teaches first grade. Not being able to see the reactions of the principal and a committee of teachers made the conversation a bit of a challenge, but the biggest challenge was a particular question. Although she had been ready for questions about what she does in the classroom, this one came as a surprise: What are three things you would *never* do as a teacher?

Afterwards Anne told me, "Mom, I've never even thought about that before." I asked, "What did you say?" She responded, "I said I try never to model behavior that I don't want see in the children, never to come to school unprepared, and never to say 'You can't learn' to a child."

This question, "What are three things you'd never do?" needs to be answered in terms of our real temptations. We won't learn ways to avoid doing harm if we give farfetched answers. As a friend, I'd never ask for a $1,000 loan. As a parent, I'd never serve only desserts at every meal. As a driver, I'd never go 100 mph on the interstate.

Reflect on the Rule

Within the realm of real possibility what would you never do? What connections do you see between this question and practicing the rule to do no harm? What are some other ways you might practice this rule? What are some ways your church, business, school, or some other institution might practice this rule?

Intentionally Doing No Harm

In *Three Simple Rules*, Rueben Job suggests some ways of practicing this rule. We can decide not to harm those with whom we disagree. These might be neighbors, co-workers, members of our church, civic leaders in our town. Job encourages us to manage conflict within groups by not gossiping about the conflict, by not speaking disparagingly of others in the conflict, by not manipulating facts, and by not diminishing those who disagree (p. 22). Job says that "laying aside our weapons" helps us "discover that we stand on common ground, inhabit a common and precious space, share a common faith, feast at a common table, and have an equal measure of God's unlimited love" (p. 23). At many funerals people facing a common loss are able to lay aside their weapons. In the face of disaster people are usually able to realize they share a common space and therefore can work for the common good. What could happen if we intentionally laid aside our weapons at other times? Practicing this rule is never easy. Job points out that it requires seeing that we share one very important gift with others whom we might dismiss or disparage: "When I commit myself to this way, I must see each person as a child of God—a recipient of love unearned, unlimited, and undeserved—just like myself" (p. 31).

Being intentional about doing no harm entails vigilance, commitment, and help from God. Job says, "Practicing our faith in the world requires our deepest resolve, our greatest faith, and our unwavering trust, and a very, very large measure of God's grace" (p. 24). In his sermon "Scriptural Christianity," John Wesley said that when we love our neighbor, we will "work no evil" against them, we will not "offend in tongue, either against justice, or against mercy or truth."[1]

> How do you respond to Job's statement that we "stand on common ground, inhabit a common and precious space, share a common faith, feast at a common table, and have an equal measure of God's unlimited love"? How might this understanding change your view of those with whom you disagree?

Reflect

Collective Harm

Among the major sources of harm that Wesley battled in the 18th century was slavery. The last letter that Wesley wrote shortly before his death was to William Wilberforce, encouraging him in his fight to end slavery. Wesley called slavery "that execrable villainy which is the scandal of religion, of England, and of human nature." Wesley wrote, "Go on, in the name of God and in the power of his might, till even American slavery (the vilest that ever saw the sun) shall vanish away before it."[2]

What Wilberforce and Wesley saw clearly was the harm that slavery caused and who was causing the harm. In this case, the "who" was the English government in its policies. Since both Wilberforce and Wesley were loyal supporters of their government, they were indirectly a part of the institution that was doing harm, and they accepted their responsibility to end that harm.

In the 21st century if we ask who or what is being harmed, the answer is overwhelming: victims of violence and war, victims of extreme poverty, the sick and injured who cannot afford medical care, workers whose wages are so low they have to go without meals or shelter, natural resources that suffer pollution, wasteful use, depletion, and destruction.

The list could go on.

At a recent conference on the environment, I saw a film about mountaintop removal in West Virginia and Kentucky in order to extract the coal within. When human beings blow up a mountain, they cannot ever restore it. Sure, they might haul in topsoil and plant grass, but the mountain is gone forever. Now when I ask myself who is responsible for this harm, I could say the greedy coal companies and standing behind them are the power companies who use the coal to make electricity. But who uses the electricity? People like me. I am complicit. Not directly, but I am a part of the system that is doing harm not only to the mountains but to the air and to the increasing number of asthmatic children who breathe it. What can I do?

The very least I can do is to conserve energy and encourage others to do the same. Beyond that I can learn all I can about alternative sources of energy and work with groups who are trying to shape public policy toward energy production that is better for the environment. I know this is a complex problem facing our world, and there are no easy answers, but I want to do no harm. I want to be a part of the solution.

Reflect

What would you add to the list of who or what is being harmed in the 21st century? What practices do you think would alleviate the harm? How might you be part of the solution?

WHAT DOES THE BIBLE SAY?

Romans 14:14-23

Paul writes to the church at Rome that "it is good not to eat meat or drink wine or do anything that makes your brother or sister stumble" (verse 21).

> Read Romans 14:14-23. What connections do you see between this Bible passage and the intentional practice of doing no harm?

Reflect on the Bible

In Romans 14, Paul outlines his stance on the tension between those who strictly observe dietary regulations grounded in their faith commitment and those who want to exercise their freedom in Christ to ignore such regulations. Paul is concerned that the quarreling about these matters disrupts community. Paul is writing to "the strong" (those who want to exercise freedom) and reminds them of their responsibility for "the weak" (probably the term used by "the strong" to characterize those who strictly observe the regulations). The strong felt free to eat the "unclean" food, that is, the food that was taboo according to Jewish dietary law. To them Paul writes, "If your brother or sister is being injured by what you eat, you are no longer walking in love" (Romans 14:15a). In other words, if your actions offend the weak, then you do harm by hurting their faith.

> How would you translate to people in the 21st century Paul's concern about not causing our brother or sister to stumble? When have you refrained from doing something that you considered perfectly ethical in order to do no harm to your sisters and brothers?

Reflect

Matthew 5:38-48

In Matthew 5, we are presented with some of the most challenging teachings of Jesus that we find in the Gospels. Before I read Walter Wink's *Engaging the Powers* I had no idea what to do with these passages, what to make of Matthew 5. It sometimes happens victims of harm have been counseled by religious leaders to turn the other cheek and go the second mile. To a victim, such advice sounds like inviting further victimization under the guise of being religious. It was a huge relief to me to read an interpretation of these passages that emphatically is not telling victims to be doormats and submit to more abuse. This interpretation gives them a dignified response that does no harm.

Reflect on the Bible

Read Matthew 5:38-48. What challenges you in this Bible reading? How does it relate to the practice of doing no harm?

Jesus' Third Way

In the NRSV, Matthew 5:39 is translated, "Do not resist an evildoer." According to Wink's interpretation, the key word to notice is "resist." The Greek word translated "resist" in the NRSV is a term for warfare, for violent conflict: *antistenai*. A translation that better captures that emphasis might be, "Do not retaliate against violence with violence," or "Do not let evil dictate the terms of your opposition." If we go with that translation, the question becomes how is it possible to counter evil. Throughout human history, most people have been able to think of only two answers: fight or flight. However, Wink says that Jesus offers us a third way, a way of "militant nonviolence" rather than a way of submission.[3]

In Matthew 5, Jesus gives his hearers, most of whom were the marginalized of society, examples of how this admonition is carried out. In the first example, they and we are told, "If anyone strikes you on the right cheek, turn the other also." To hear this in an empowering way, it is important to know a few things about cultural customs of Jesus' day:

Equals who strike each other do so with their fists.

To strike someone with your fist is to suggest that your opponent is your equal.

If you are to strike someone, you do so with your right hand; your left hand is used for unclean things.

People with power strike their underlings with the back of their right hands in order to insult them.[4]

Now let's look again at this teaching to turn the other cheek. What Jesus is describing here is not a potential fight between equals, but an insult, delivered by a person of greater power to a person of lesser power. Thus, he might be describing a master striking a slave or a Roman officer striking a Jewish civilian. Why might we think this is an insult? Because this is not a blow delivered by someone's right fist. If it were, it would land on the opponent's left cheek. To deliver a right-handed blow to someone's right cheek requires using the back of one's hand, and that action is an insult intended to humiliate, not to injure. A person would not backhand a peer, only an underling.[5]

Since Jesus' hearers were mainly persons without power, they were more often than not the victims of insult, not the deliverers of insult. So why was Jesus telling people accustomed to humiliation to turn the other cheek? Wink argues that he was showing them a nonviolent response, a way of robbing the offender of the power to humiliate. The person who turned the other cheek was saying: Go ahead and hit me again. You didn't insult me the first time. There's no way you are going to humiliate me.[6] This response throws strikers off balance. They can't use their left hands. If they use the right hand to hit the left cheek, they are making the victims their equals. The person who tries to insult someone of lesser power is put into an awkward bind. At the very least this response gives dignity to the recipient of the blow. At best this response gives the offender pause to reflect, and perhaps the offender will be persuaded of error and repent. Both parties stand to be more whole as the result of this encounter. This is not retaliation and it is not flight; rather this is Jesus' third way.[7]

The second example that Jesus gives occurs in a court of law where a creditor is suing a debtor. The background for understanding this situation is to be found in Deuteronomy 10. If a creditor loans money to neighbors who are so poor that their only collateral is their outer garments, then the creditors must return the garments each evening so that the poor debtors have clothing in which to sleep. In Jesus' example, the borrower is too poor to repay the loan and the creditor is taking this poor person to court.[8]

Again, remember that Jesus' audience is made up primarily of poor people. They hate the Roman system that takes away their land, their possessions, and eventually their outer garments. Jesus is telling them that if they are taken to court because they can't repay a loan, they should give over their inner garments—their underwear—as well. He is telling them to take off all their clothes and walk out of the room stark naked.[9]

What's going on here? It's important to know that public nakedness was taboo in Jesus' society. That may not startle us, but what is amazing to the modern reader is that the shame of public nakedness did not belong to the naked, but to the one who saw or caused the nakedness. Here again, Jesus is illustrating a nonviolent way of responding to an oppressor, a way that would cause profound humiliation. Jesus was telling his hearers to say, "You want my cloak. Here, have my underwear too!" By stripping naked, the debtor has made the creditor break Jewish law and in a nonviolent way, has unmasked a rotten system. In addition, the debtor has given the creditor an opportunity to take responsibility for bad behavior and change direction.[10]

The third of Jesus' examples of nonviolent opposition is similar in its intended effect. In understanding this one, it is important to know that the Roman government had a law forbidding Roman soldiers from making civilians carry the soldiers' packs more than a mile. There were mile markers along Roman roads to encourage the soldiers to follow this law. Apparently the reason for the law was not so much to protect the backs of civilians as they shouldered packs weighing upwards of eighty pounds. It was to quell the anger of the civilians who might otherwise be tempted to report the soldiers who would then incur heavy fines.[11]

Here Jesus is not telling the subjugated to revolt. Instead, he is saying, "Go the second mile." The surprised soldier would be dumbfounded. Why is this Jew offering, without a hint of complaint, to take my pack another mile? Is this an insult? Is this person trying to get me in trouble for breaking the law? Again, Jesus' counsel is to seize the initiative and throw the soldier off balance. This causes no harm. In fact, the soldier may be given a chance to reconsider and repent.[12]

Reflect

How do you respond to Walter Wink's interpretation of the difficult passages in Matthew 5? What challenges you or makes you curious? Do you agree or disagree with his interpretations? Why?

Retaliation or Not?

Having looked at these difficult passages, let's return to the question: what do they have to do with the admonition to "do no harm"? When we retaliate, returning evil for evil, harm for harm, a cycle of harm is put into motion, a cycle that is difficult to stop. When we respond to evil in ways that surprise and befuddle, we are much less likely to do harm to ourselves (by being a doormat) and to others (by seeking vengeance). We are even offering the offender the opportunity to pause long enough to take another path, rather than to continue on the path of sinful oppression. If we truly believe that those who harm us are God's beloved children, just as we are, why not give them a chance to change? As Walter Wink says, our choice of loving confrontation can free us from docile submission that kills our spirits while freeing the oppressor from sin.[13] Even if nonviolent resistance doesn't change the oppressor, it gives the oppressed a sense of dignity and self-respect. Standing up for oneself in a nonviolent way is a path to confidence, courage, and strength to face the inevitable foes we'll encounter further down the road.

Walter Wink's interpretation of this difficult part of Matthew may never be widely accepted. It flies in the face of what many of us have been taught—to be vengeful or to be nice and put a lid on the anger that we feel when we or our loved ones have been violated. However, this interpretation addresses the skepticism that many people have about turning the other cheek and going the second mile as realistic, humanly possible ways of responding to hurt, violence, and resultant harm. Another way to think about these teachings is that the instructions from Jesus are directed toward the one who must respond to the harm being done instead of the one doing the harm. Jesus gives a better way that carries a potential for good for them and for the oppressor.

> Recall times when you have not retaliated. What were your motives for not seeking revenge? In these times were you able to preserve your own dignity and self-respect? Can you anticipate some situations in the near future when you may be tempted to retaliate?

Reflect

CLOSING – A GUIDE FOR DAILY PRAYER

Welcoming God's Presence

God of justice and mercy, you want us to love our enemies and to do them no harm. Forgive us when we fail, and help us to practice that kind of love. Amen.

Scripture

Happy are those
  who do not follow the advice of the wicked,
or take the path that sinners tread,
  or sit in the seat of scoffers;
but their delight is in the law of the LORD,
  and on his law they meditate day and night.
— Psalm 1:1-2

Meditation

Reflect on Psalm 1:1-2 in terms of the admonition to do no harm. Write down your insights from this reflection:

Prayer

Pray for the power and courage to do no harm and to intercede for the victims of harm.

Blessing

Those who do no harm "are like trees
  planted by streams of water,
which yield their fruit in its season,
  and their leaves do not wither."
— Psalm 1:3a

---

[1] John Wesley, "Scriptural Christianity," Sermon 4 (text from the 1872 edition - Thomas Jackson, editor). From website of The United Methodist Church; http://new.gbgm-umc.org/umhistory/wesley/sermons/4/.

[2] John Wesley, "Letter to William Wilberforce," February 24, 1791. From website of the UMC; http://gbgm-umc.org/umw/wesley/wilber.stm.

[3] Walter Wink, "Reclaiming Jesus' Nonviolent Alternative," *The Living Pulpit* (October-December 1998); p. 40.

[4] Wink; p. 40.

[5] Wink; p. 40.

[6] Wink; p. 40.

[7] Wink; p. 40.

[8] Wink; pp. 40–41.

[9] Wink; p. 41.

[10] Wink; p. 41.

[11] Wink; p. 41.

[12] Wink; pp. 41–42.

[13] Wink; p. 42.

Chapter

Do Good –
Understanding the Rule

Focus Question:

Most of us think of ourselves as good people. What does it mean to do good?

A Prayer

Holy God, open our eyes that we may see what good needs doing; open our imaginations that we may figure out what good we can do; and open our hearts to your empowering love that we may have the courage to act. Through Christ we pray. Amen.

WHAT DOES THE RULE SAY?

Bread or No Bread

"You mean free bread?" I hear the clerk ask. "We don't give away free bread." I was lost in my thoughts as I sat by a window in a bakery with my laptop and a cup of coffee writing this very chapter on what it means to do good. The clerk's voice caught my attention. I looked up and saw a small boy walk out the door and get into an old car in which there is another small boy and a woman, presumably their mother. As she pulled the car away from the curb, I saw the back seat is full of their belongings. Then I heard one clerk say to another, "Yeah, she sent the little boy in instead of coming herself."

Just the week before I had written a piece on homelessness, and four weeks before that I did research on hunger in America. There I was with a computer filled with statistics about poverty and beside it a loaf of bread for dinner that evening. What does it mean to do good in a world where some people—and I am one of them—take it for granted that there will be bread on the table tonight and others, like that family of three, take it for granted that there probably will be no bread? In the first two weeks of this study, we examined our lives to find ways to avoid doing harm. Now we turn to the second rule—do good—and look at what it means for our lives.

Reflect on the Rule

Quickly jot down a list of ten ways to do good. Then reflect on your list. What do these ten ways tell you about what "doing good" means to you? Which of these ways involve you as the actor? Which involve you along with other people? Which do not involve you at all?

Seeing the Need

The second simple rule—do good—is harder to practice than it may sound. To do good requires seeing the need and taking action. Rueben Job calls doing good "a proactive way of living." It is not necessary to wait to be asked to help. "I do not need to wait until circumstances cry out for aid to relieve suffering or correct some horrible injustice. I can decide that my way of living will come down on the side of doing good to all in every circumstance and in every way I can" (*Three Simple Rules*; pp. 37–38).

It is hard for us to see the needs of others when our focus is so often on what we call our needs. We live in a culture in which the constant message from the marketplace is "you need this." A hundred years ago most towns and villages in the United States had stores with essential goods: food staples, cloth, hardware, farm supplies. My grandparents never thought they needed any more than that. My grandmother made clothes for the family, and my grandfather built the furniture in the house. Their farm animals and garden supplied the food on their table. While I am not suggesting that we can or should return to that way of living, I describe their life to raise the question of the meaning of need.

In our consumerist culture we often identify as needs our desires of more things and experiences that are not necessities for living. Thus, it has become acceptable to many to take much more than their share of the earth's resources. As Job says, we live in "a culture in which this world's treasures are rapidly gravitating away from those who desperately need a reasonable share of those treasures to survive." We live in "a climate in which it has become easy to turn away from the social and economic injustice that does immense harm to many and provides rich benefits to few" (p. 46).

We are a part of it, and those things we think we need help to shape both our culture and ourselves. As Job writes, "Far too many times we have contributed to a competitive culture that encourages greed and selfishness and discourages compassion, sharing, fairness, and commitment to the common good" (p. 46). Commitment to the common good entails seeing what other people need instead of focusing on our selfish desires for more and more.

> What do you really need? Which of your needs could you really do without? What does the marketplace tell you about what you need? Does the world of advertising and consumerism ever address what the community needs? Who or what is looking out for the common good?
>
> **Reflect**

Your Deep Gladness and the World's Deep Hunger

Frederick Buechner, writer and Presbyterian minister, offers this often quoted guidance about discerning vocation: "The place God calls you to is the place where your deep gladness and the world's deep hunger meet."[1]

31

Here Buechner is talking about two important kinds of need: our need to use our talents and "deep gladness" and the needs of the world. When we find that intersection, we have found God's call to us to do good.

> **Reflect**
>
> What are your talents? What gives you a sense of deep gladness? What needs in your community might benefit from them?

That intersection for John Wesley brought him to work with the poor. His "great gladness" was preaching the gospel of God's love; and when he saw people in need, he knew that their suffering must be addressed before the good news would have meaning. He saw needs of the poor through his constant acquaintance with their situation. Although he preached to them in open fields and market places, he intentionally made regular visits with them and required people of the Methodist movement to do the same.

Because he knew the condition of the poor, he could argue against a "wickedly, devilishly false" conclusion that the poor were poor because they didn't work.[2] Wesley wrote, "One great reason why the rich in general have so little sympathy for the poor, is, because they so seldom visit them."[3]

Because of his awareness of the plight of the poor, Wesley found a variety of ways to do good for the poor. Members of class meetings took up collections for the needy; and Wesley himself went door to door to solicit funds for food, fuel, and clothing. Out of his concern for the sick, he also required that members of classes and societies visit them.[4] Wesley's work with the poor went beyond charity. Wanting to help the poor help themselves, he organized health clinics, cooperatives, and credit unions. He wrote and published cheap tracts and abridgments.[5] He was concerned about the education of both children and adults.

Ted Jennings writes that "Wesley sought to make the welfare of the poor the criterion of every aspect of the Methodist movement." Even in the building of meeting places he had the poor in mind. They were to be built as economically as possible so that Methodists would not be beholden to the rich.[6]

> Let all preaching-houses be built plain and decent; but not more expensive than is absolutely unavoidable. Otherwise the necessity of raising money will make rich men necessary to us. But if so, we must be dependent upon them, yea and governed by them. And then farewell all Methodist discipline, if not doctrine too. (*Large Minutes* VIII; p. 332)[7]

Today many Christians tend to understand stewardship as supporting the church budget, but Wesley believed we are to be stewards for God and for the poor. He understood that everything we have is a gift from God, and that anything that is surplus is to be given to the poor. Keeping our surplus for ourselves is problematic for Christians: it leads to pride and selfishness, and it violates the rights of the poor. He didn't use the word *consumerism*, but that is what he was criticizing. "Everything about thee which cost more than Christian duty required thee to lay out is the blood of the poor" (*On Dress* VII; p. 21).[8]

How do you respond to Wesley's ideas about doing good and helping the poor? What challenges you? Why? What appeals to you? Why?

Reflect

Doing Good and God's Grace

The reasons for doing good are connected to Wesley's understanding of grace. God's grace goes before us, making possible our knowledge of God. Wesley called this prevenient grace (from Latin words meaning "going before"). Through justifying grace, God forgives our sins and restores us to right relationship. Sanctifying grace continues throughout our lives; it is God's work within us to make us whole (in Wesley's terms, to bring about holiness in our lives). To Wesley, salvation was not a result of our efforts but of God's initiative. Thus, doing good is not a means to salvation, but the natural response to God's love and grace. The response of faithful discipleship is love of God and neighbor—an active love embodied in what Wesley called "works of mercy."

For Wesley these works of mercy included:

> . . . every thing which we give, or speak, or do, whereby our neighbour may be profited; whereby another man may receive any advantage, either in his body or soul. The feeding the hungry, the clothing the naked, the entertaining or assisting the stranger, the visiting those that are sick or in prison, the comforting the afflicted, the instructing the ignorant, the reproving the wicked, the exhorting and encouraging the well-doer; and if there be any other work of mercy, it is equally included in this direction.[9]

Reflect

What connections do you see between doing good and God's grace?

WHAT DOES THE BIBLE SAY?

Throughout Scripture the admonition to do good is a persistent theme expressed in a variety of ways.

Reflect on the Bible

Read each of the following Bible passages. How do they help you define what it means to do good?

Exodus 20:12-17

Leviticus 19:18

The Great Commandment in Matthew 22:37-40; Mark 12:28-33; and Luke 10:27

Micah 6:6-8

James 1:19-27; 2:14-17

In the Ten Commandments (Exodus 20:1-17) and in the multitude of laws of Deuteronomy and Leviticus, there are many that concern ethical treatment of other people. In Leviticus 19:18 we find a basic principle of doing good: "You shall not take vengeance or bear a grudge against any of your people, but you shall love your neighbour as yourself: I am the LORD." This principle is repeated by Jesus in Matthew 19:19 in his conversation with the rich young man about keeping the commandments and in the Great Commandment in Matthew 22:37-40; Mark 12:28-33; and Luke 10:27.

In Proverbs 31:1-9 we find the wisdom taught to King Lemuel by his mother. In verses 8-9, we find that it is the obligation of those who have power to advocate for the most vulnerable in society:

> Speak out for those who cannot speak,
>   for the rights of all the destitute.
> Speak out, judge righteously,
>   defend the rights of the poor and needy.

In Micah 6:6-8 a questioner asks, What can I bring to restore my relationship with God? What kind of sacrifice will be acceptable to God? Then the questioner offers three proposals of sacrificial offerings, none of which answer the question. Indeed, the question changes to an inquiry about what is good. Then, it is clear that what God wants is not an offering but action: to do justice, to love mercy, and to walk humbly with God. As the prophet Micah presents this question and answer, it is as if Israel is asking the question. Biblical scholar James L. Mays contends that this passage does not seem to be addressed to a specific situation, but rather is a "more general and final statement," as if it has the weight of tradition behind it.[10] Mays says that these are not three separate acts but interconnected: doing justice is based on a sense of mutuality with those in need, and this love of mercy comes from walking humbly with God.[11]

Next we look at two passages from the letter of James (1:19-27; 2:14-17). In James 1:19-27, we read the admonition that Christians are to "be doers of the word, and not merely hearers who deceive themselves" (verse 22). Wesley comments on James 1:27, which says that the practice of "pure religion" is to visit the orphans and widows and be "spotless before God." He says, "But this cannot be done till we have given our hearts to God, and love our neighbors as ourselves."[12] In James 2:14-17, the writer addresses what has become a long-standing controversy—faith versus works:

> What good is it, my brothers and sisters, if you say you have faith but do not have works? Can faith save you? If a brother or sister is naked and lacks

daily food, and one of you says to them, "Go in peace; keep warm and eat your fill," and yet you do not supply their bodily needs, what is the good of that? So faith by itself, if it has no works, is dead.

Wesley says that James does not argue against Paul's doctrine of grace but against the error of abusing this doctrine. In his *New Testament Notes* he says, "'Works do not give life to faith, but faith begets work, and then is perfected by them' (James 2:22)."[13]

Reflect

In your experience, how does faith lead to works? How has your faith led you to do good?

CLOSING – A GUIDE FOR DAILY PRAYER

Welcoming God's Presence

God of love and grace, help us to see our neighbors' needs and to respond in acts of love and mercy. In Christ's name we pray. Amen.

Scripture

"For by grace you have been saved through faith, and this is not your own doing; it is the gift of God—not the result of works, so that no one may boast. For we are what he has made us, created in Christ Jesus for good works, which God prepared beforehand to be our way of life."
— Ephesians 2:8-10

Meditation

Reflect on Ephesians 2:8-10 in terms of the admonition to do good. Write down your insights from this reflection. How have the Scripture readings in Chapter 3, as well as the illustrations and reflections, shaped your concept of what it is to do good?

Prayer

Pray for the ability to see where you can do good, how you can use your resources for the tasks, and for the courage to follow through. Pray for God's intention for justice and mercy in the situations where you see the need for justice, mercy, healing, and peace.

Blessing

"Happy are those who observe justice,
  who do righteousness at all times."
                                        — Psalm 106:3

---

[1] Frederick Buechner, *Wishful Thinking: A Theological ABC* (Harper & Row, 1973); p. 95.
[2] Theodore W. Jennings Jr., "Wesley's Preferential Option for the Poor," in *Quarterly Review* (Fall 1989); p. 14.
[3] Quoted in Jennings; p. 14.
[4] Sondra Wheeler, "John Wesley and 'Social Ethics.'" From the website of The Project on Lived Theology at the University of Virginia; www.livedtheology.org/pdfs.
[5] Jennings; p. 15.
[6] Jennings; pp. 15–16.
[7] Quoted in Jennings; p. 16.
[8] Quoted in Jennings; p. 19.
[9] John Wesley, "Upon Our Lord's Sermon on the Mount, 6," Sermon 26 (from the 1874 edition, Thomas Jackson, ed.); http://new.gbgm-umc.org/umhistory/wesley/sermons/26.
[10] James L. Mays, *Micah: A Commentary* (SCM Press LTD, 1976); p. 138.
[11] Mays; p.142.
[12] Quoted in Gregory S. Clapper, "*Orthokardia*: The Practical Theology of John Wesley's Heart Religion," *Quarterly Review* (Spring 1990); p. 55.
[13] Quoted in Clapper; p. 54.

Chapter 4

Do Good –
Practicing the Rule

Focus Question:

How can we put into practice the rule of doing good? What difference can our actions make in our own lives and in the lives of others?

A Prayer

Everlasting God, as we put into practice this rule of doing good, show us the way past our doubts and fears, and give us confidence and resolve to make a difference. In Christ's name. Amen.

WHAT DOES THE RULE SAY?

In your congregation and community you probably can think of dozens of ways to practice the rule to do good —visiting the sick, volunteering in schools, supplying the food pantry, serving on town council, caring for children, and being a responsible citizen.

However, like the first rule, this one is harder to practice than it may sound. Besides seeing the need and being proactive, doing good requires confronting our doubts and persevering in the face of rejection.

> **Reflect on the Rule**
>
> What are some ways you have practiced the rule to do good? What challenges have you identified in your efforts to practice this rule?

Anathoth Community Garden

Less than twenty miles northwest of the University of North Carolina at Chapel Hill in rural Orange County is Anathoth Community Garden. Determined not "to repay evil for evil," the community surrounding Cedar Grove United Methodist Church planted this garden and thus practiced of the rule of doing good. "The garden began with the murder of Bill King in 2003. Bill, a white man whose wife was black, was shot at his bait and tackle shop; and many thought the murder was racially motivated. The uneasy truce between blacks and whites in this small farming community seemed ready to snap. Blame was cast, and some people wanted revenge," recalls Fred Bahnson, the garden manager.[1]

The spring following the murder, Grace Hackney, the pastor of Cedar Grove, met Valee Taylor, an African-American who is a long-time member of the Cedar Grove community and friend of Bill King, at the post office beside the church and began talking. "Valee told me I was the first white pastor to stop to speak to him. I told him to let me know if I could ever do anything to help him and pointed out the parsonage. Three months later he knocked on the door and the idea for the vigil was birthed."

About 100 people from the community attended the prayer vigil that Hackney organized. Later Taylor told Hackney that his mother, a descendant of an African-American sharecropper, had had a vision of giving five acres to the community for some kind of mission. "He said during the prayer vigil she had been told that we were the ones to give the land to," said Hackney. The Cedar Grove congregation already had been talking about responsible use of land. One idea was a community garden where people could learn organic gardening, care for creation, and provide food for the hungry.

This idea meshed with a series of community conversations that Hackney started in order to address the poverty in which the racial tensions were rooted. Cedar Grove was an agricultural community, but many households either didn't have enough food or else ate food laden with empty calories. Hackney says, "The new look of poverty was obesity; and it seemed sinful that with access to land, there would be people without affordable access to healthy food."

Taylor's mother donated her land to Cedar Grove UMC, and plans were made for Anathoth Community Garden. Membership is open to anyone in the area for $5 per season and weekly work in the garden. It isn't divided into plots for single families. Instead, everyone works in the whole garden. They grow enough produce to share with the poor in the community who cannot work there. The garden is also tended by Volunteers for Youth, a program through which teenagers can fulfill community service hours by working in the garden. Hackney says, "In a day when a lot of things make God weep— war, climate change—we're blessed to be engaged in a way of living that must make God smile." Cedar Grove UMC and members of Anathoth Community Garden are practicing the second of the three simple rules—do good.[2]

> What potential positive effects for good do you see in the story of the Anathoth Community Garden? What are some of the unseen benefits to the community? What potential exists in your community for a community garden?
>
> **Reflect**

The Fear of Doing Good

As Rueben Job points out, one obstacle to doing good is the fear of being overwhelmed by the vast amount of need out there. What difference can I make? In a world of poverty, mistrust, depleting natural resources, and violence, what good can I do? Where do I start? Once I begin, how much good is enough? What if my doing good gets out of control? Where are the limits of my time, energy, and money? What if my doing good conflicts with other commitments I have made? (*Three Simple Rules*; p. 39).

> **Reflect**
>
> What questions would you add to the list of fears?

This story of a young woman in New York City is an encouragement to those of us who wonder whether we can make a real difference. Amanda Block, a public relations professional, was already doing good through her work in the emergency food program at Washington Square United Methodist Church (now merged with another congregation to become the United Methodist Church of the Village) when she discovered another way she could make a difference. She spent hours each Sunday in conversation with the meal guests. They told her about other places where they could find food and about the difficulties they often had in meeting basic needs. Believing that knowledge is power, Amanda set out to empower street people to find what they need.

Amanda left her career in public relations to dedicate all of her time to a project designed to provide information to the most needy. She did more research and began compiling information into what she called Street Sheets. Over the next several years the sheets evolved from being a listing of food services to four different brochures on services (hygiene, medical/legal, shelter, and food) for the poor of New York City. Printed so that they can be easily copied, they provide the names, addresses, and other information about available services.

> **Reflect**
>
> How do you respond to the story of Amanda Block and Street Sheets? Have you ever seen the opportunity to do good but were overwhelmed with the extent of need? How did you respond? If you were able to go forward with your efforts, what empowered you?

Rueben Job says that sometimes we are reluctant to do good because of fear that our efforts may be "rejected, ridiculed, and misused" (*Three Simple*

Rules; p. 40). Rejection of our efforts may range from simply being ignored to outright opposition. Have you had the experience of bringing an idea for a mission project to your church council where it was shelved in favor of some other project? Have you spoken up in the workplace against a sexist or racist joke and then suffered social ostracism because of your stand? Have you advocated for legislation that would serve the common good only to have the bill killed in committee? Such experiences can dampen our enthusiasm in a hurry.

However, Job writes that the "desire to do good is not limited by the thoughts or actions of others" (p. 40). Sometimes we confuse what is within our control and what is not. It is within my control to choose to do good. Others' response to my good deed is not within my control. Job writes, "And the reward for my doing good is not cancelled or diminished by the response to my acts of goodness. I will have the reward of knowing I did what was right and pleasing to God" (pp. 40–41). Rueben Job reminds us that for John Wesley "'the image of God fresh stamped on the heart'" is the reward of faithfulness as we seek to do good (p. 42). At times we will make a difference in the lives of others, but whether accepted or rejected, the good we attempt to do always makes a difference in our own lives.

> Have there been times you have retreated from doing good because of fear of rejection and ridicule? Can you recall times when you chose to do good in the face of rejection? If so, what empowered you?
>
> **Reflect**

Some may hear the rule to do good as *unhealthy* self-denial. As Job points out, our culture keeps telling us to put ourselves first, and often that message is a part of marketing strategy to sell us more things. However, following this rule leads to *healthy* self-denial. Job writes, "To love God with all of life and to love neighbor as self is not to denigrate, deny, or devalue self. It is . . . to place enormous value on self and on neighbor. It is to choose to live in the reign of God NOW" (pp. 46–47). That is the difference following this rule makes in our lives—we are choosing this day to live in God's new order of love, peace, and wholeness.

WHAT DOES THE BIBLE SAY?

The Bible is consistent in its message about the practice of doing good as a key expression of our relationship with God and neighbor.

Reflect on the Bible

Prayerfully read the following Scriptures and write notes about the ways they speak to you about the practice of doing good. How do they inspire you to practice doing good?

1 John 3:17-18

Romans 12

Galatians 5:22–6:2

1 John 3:17-18

"Our church has an unwritten rule: we will never ignore a member's basic need," writes Stan Wilson, pastor of Northside Baptist in Clinton, Mississippi. He says he knows his congregation will not let a member go without food, medical care, or shelter; but he couldn't get them to put it in writing. "Why not make it official?" He tells about the Church of the Servant King in Eugene, Oregon, which has made it official. "The members claim that this rule has freed them in surprising ways. They work fewer hours so they can spend more time with one another; they are able to afford to work less because they know they can count on each other." Wilson suspects that the fear of someone taking advantage of the church keeps them from saying out loud that they will never ignore a member's basic need. He says that the writer of 1 John didn't have that fear: "How does God's love abide in anyone who has the world's goods and sees a brother or sister in need and yet refuses help? Little children, let us love, not in word or speech, but in truth and action" (1 John 3:17-18).[3]

Would your congregation never ignore a brother or sister's basic need? Would they put their commitment in writing? Would you personally make that kind of commitment?

Reflect

Romans 12

In Romans 12, Paul has much to say about how we can practice doing good. In the Christian community, we don't have to feel overwhelmed by the need we see. We don't have to think that we need to tackle a problem all by ourselves. Thinking with "sober judgement" will remind us that we can rely on the differing gifts of our brothers and sisters in Christ. Paul writes, "For as in one body we have many members, and not all the members have the same function, so we, who are many, are one body in Christ, and individually we are members one of another. We have gifts that differ according to the grace given to us" (Romans 12:4-6a).

This chapter of Romans describes how God's grace can transform our lives. Because Christians have been adopted into the family of God, they are to shape their lives accordingly. Romans 12:3-13 admonishes the Christian community about how to respond to God's grace in Christ. They are able to do good and to enact their faith as they value each other's gifts to the community and promote unity.

Paul describes examples of the kinds of gifts that are to be used for the glory of God and the common good. As Paul J. Achtemeier points out, this is not an exhaustive list. It is not exactly the same list that Paul describes in 1 Corinthians 12. Paul makes clear that there are no superior gifts and thus no cause for pride and the discord it can produce. Paul also stresses that his admonitions are not ways to earn God's love, but appropriate responses to the grace we already have received. Our good deeds are responses to grace, not ways of earning grace.[4]

Romans 12:14-21 describes how God's grace shapes our dealings beyond the Christian community as well. Paul has written first about how unity is the form in which grace transforms life within the Christian community.

Now he turns to peace as the form in which grace shapes the Christian's relationships beyond that community. His admonitions are examples of ways to live in peace. Be humble. Do not seek revenge. Verses 20-21 are often misunderstood in this regard. Offering peace to enemies is a way to turn around their lives. When Paul speaks doing good to enemies, he is quoting Proverbs 25:22 and saying such behavior burns away hate and turns enemies into friends.[5]

> **Reflect**
>
> What gifts do you see in the people of your church community? How are these gifts used to practice doing good? How can you use your gifts for the practice of doing good? How do you think the community outside your church is affected by using your gifts to do good?

Galatians 5:22–6:2

Paul's letter to the Galatians asserts that Christians need to hold together grace and works. Major themes in this letter are the relationship between law and grace and the nature of Christian freedom. Paul feared that a segment of the Galatian community was promoting obedience to the law rather than grace as the means of salvation, and he argued that God's gift of new relationship in Christ is what both evokes our good works and makes them possible. In Galatians 5:22–6:1, Paul says that life in the Spirit, the life transformed by grace, results in the fruit of the Spirit: "love, joy, peace, patience, kindness, generosity, faithfulness, gentleness, and self-control" (5:22-23a).

When a member of the community is involved in wrongdoing, Christians are to "restore such a one in a spirit of gentleness" (Galatians 6:1). Paul writes that by bearing one another's burdens, we "will fulfill the law of Christ" (6:2). It is grace that empowers the practice of doing good, which in turn, transforms the community.

How has your Christian community been shaped by grace? How has grace transformed the deeds of the community? How has grace shaped your community's efforts to do good in the larger society?

Reflect

CLOSING — A GUIDE FOR DAILY PRAYER

Welcoming God's Presence

God of gentleness and love, through the ages you have empowered your people to do good. In a world which overwhelms us with opportunities to do good, show us how to make a difference. In Christ's name we pray. Amen.

Scripture

"Bless those who persecute you; bless and do not curse them. Rejoice with those who rejoice, weep with those who weep. Live in harmony with one another; do not be haughty, but associate with the lowly; do not claim to be wiser than you are. Do not repay anyone evil for evil, but take thought for what is noble in the sight of all. If it is possible, so far as it depends on you, live peaceably with all."

— Romans 12:14-18

Meditation

Reflect on Romans 12:14-18 in terms of the admonition to do good. Write down your insights from this reflection. How have the Scripture readings in Chapter 4, as well as the illustrations and reflections, influenced your ideas about how to do good?

Prayer

During this Lenten season pray for the ability to see ways you can do good, to have the power to act and make a difference, and to rest in the assurance that your desire to do good is not limited by the response of others.

Blessing

Today live in love, holding fast to what is good. Be a blessing to enemies as well as friends. Overcome evil with good, and make a difference in the world that God loves.

---

[1] Fred Bahnson, "Compost for the Kingdom," *Christian Century* (September 5, 2006).
[2] Interview with Grace Hackney, June 22, 2008. Background material from Bahnson's essays "Compost for the Kingdom" and "A Garden Becomes a Protest: The Field at Anathoth," *Orion* (July/August 2007). Further background material from Dawn Baumgartner Vaughan, "Bountiful Harvest," *The Herald-Sun* (May 26, 2007).
[3] Stan Wilson, "Living by the Word: Ties That Bind," *Christian Century* (May 2, 2006).
[4] Paul J. Achtemeier, *Romans, Interpretation: A Bible Commentary for Teaching and Preaching* (John Knox Press, 1985); pp. 196–200.
[5] Achtemeier; pp. 201–202.

Chapter

Stay in Love With God —
Understanding the Rule

Focus Question:

Christians love God. What does it mean to stay in love with God?

A Prayer

O God, the source of our being, we know you love us, and yet we don't always do our part to stay in touch. Help us to be formed in the disciplines that will keep us in loving relationship with you. In Christ's name. Amen.

WHAT DOES THE RULE SAY?

As Rueben Job says, while the first two rules are important, they are difficult to sustain if we don't also practice the third rule—stay in love with God.

Reflect on the Rule

What is your initial impression of the rule to stay in love with God? What images or ideas come to your mind when you hear this rule?

Life Disciplines

As a child I took piano lessons and practiced every day. By the end of high school, I had learned to play some fairly difficult music. Later, I played only occasionally; but when I became a pastor of rural churches, often I'd be the only person in worship who could play. Some Sundays I nearly tripped over my robe after trying to receive the offering with proper dignity and then get to the piano in time to play the Doxology.

After a particularly difficult season of life when I sorely needed renewal, I realized I needed regular discipline—something totally different. Then it occurred to me that all those piano lessons and years of practice had provided me with more than the ability to play the piano. They had been a discipline that had held me steady through the challenges of growing up, and they could again be that grounding force.

Disciplines order our lives so that we remember what is important. John Wesley led a highly disciplined life and expected his followers to do the same. Even though "Methodist" was first a derisive name that Oxford students used for the Holy Club, the word accurately described the lifestyle of early Methodists. To stay in love with God, John Wesley firmly believed that Christians must "methodically" observe certain spiritual disciplines that he called ordinances, or means of grace.

Reflect

What disciplines are you currently observing in your own life? What disciplines have you observed in the past? What challenges or benefits resulted from these disciplines?

Spiritual Disciplines as Means of Grace

Rueben Job in *Three Simple Rules* enumerates some essential spiritual disciplines, or practices, as John Wesley saw them: "a daily time of prayer; reflection upon and study of Scripture; regular participation in the life of a Christian community, including weekly worship and regular participation in the Lord's Supper; doing some act of goodness or mercy; and taking opportunities to share with and learn from others who also seek to follow the way of Jesus" (pp. 55–56). In the General Rules, Wesley's list of ordinances added "fasting or abstinence."[1] In other lists of "means of grace" he would add works of mercy.[2] Job reminds us that Wesley "saw that the consistent practice of these spiritual disciplines kept those who sought to follow Christ in touch with the presence and power of Christ so they could fulfill their desire to live as faithful disciples" (pp. 53–54). Christians through the ages have found these practices to be essential to loving God and neighbor. In this chapter we'll be looking at these disciplines—prayer, worship, the Lord's Supper, Bible reading and study, and fasting—in terms of what they meant to John Wesley and the Methodist tradition. In Chapter 6, we will consider how we might practice these disciplines in our own lives.

Which discipline or "means of grace" appeals most to you? Why? How do you respond to the idea that consistent practice of these disciplines keeps us in touch with Christ's presence and power?

Reflect

Prayer

Steve Harper in *Devotional Life in the Wesleyan Tradition* writes that it is no exaggeration to say that Wesley "lived to pray and prayed to live."[3] Wesley called prayer "the grand means of drawing near to God."[4] Based on his understanding of the Christian faith as living in relationship to God through Jesus Christ, prayer was the way of maintaining that relationship. For private prayer, Wesley's habit for over fifty years was to rise at 4:30 or

5:00 A.M. so that his first thoughts would focus on God. He ordered his prayers in several ways: following a weekly pattern with a topic for each day and using written prayers in which he would place parentheses to remind him where to use extemporaneous prayers. His diary tells us that in addition to morning prayers, he would use the changing of the hour to pray throughout the day. In the evening, Wesley's prayer time was a review of the day in which he made confession, resolved to make amendments, and entrusted himself to the care of God for the night.[5]

For Wesley public prayer was also essential. He observed morning and evening prayer with others, sometimes in small groups and other times in Anglican parish churches. In private and public prayer he used *The Book of Common Prayer*, the historic prayers of the church, and prayers written by his contemporaries.[6]

Reflect

How do you respond to Wesley's discipline for personal and public prayer? Does it appeal to you? Why or why not?

Worship and the Lord's Supper

When Wesley organized the early Methodists into classes, bands, and societies, he made sure that their meetings did not conflict with Sunday worship in Anglican churches.[7] He also scheduled and designed Methodist preaching services so that his followers would not substitute them for Holy Communion in their parish churches.[8] John Wesley had no patience with people who thought they could live as Christians without being in community. He wrote, " 'Holy solitaries' is a phrase no more consistent with the gospel than holy adulterers. The gospel of Christ knows of no religion, but social; no holiness but social holiness."[9] Life in Christ means a life lived in the body of Christ.

John Wesley received Communion usually twice a week during his adult life. In his sermon "The Duty of Constant Communion," he declared that "it is the duty of every Christian to receive the Lord's Supper as often as he can."[10] When asked what we are participating in when we receive the bread and cup, Wesley emphasized that the Hebraic word for remembrance (Luke 22:19—"Do this in remembrance of me.") is more than recollection. It means recalling an event so completely that it is made present to us. Because of this emphasis Wesley spoke of the *real presence* of Christ in the meal. When we receive the bread and cup, the risen Christ is present.[11]

Wesley scholar Albert Outler writes that Wesley saw the Lord's Supper as "the paradigm of *all* 'the means of grace'—the chief actual means of actual grace and, as such, literally indispensable in the Christian life."[12] Because Wesley saw the Lord's Supper as the means of prevenient, justifying, and sanctifying grace, Methodists have practiced open Communion.[13] All people are welcome at Christ's table. No one is excluded.

> What is your experience of the Lord's Supper? How do you experience the presence and power of Christ when you take the bread and the cup?
>
> **Reflect**

Bible Reading and Study

John Wesley referred to himself as *homo unis libri*—a man of one book. Although he read widely, he saw the Bible as having a unique ability to bring people to encounter God. For devotional purposes he read the Bible slowly. He read in the early morning hours and late in the evening—times when he could be alone to meditate on what he read.[14] As a systematic reader of the Bible, Wesley followed the daily readings in the *Book of Common Prayer*. This way, he was able to read the Old Testament once per year and the New Testament more than once. He made notes and used the best study aids available in his day. Wesley even prepared notes to share with others who had not had the access to education that had been afforded him at Oxford.[15]

For Wesley, the discipline of reading the Bible was corporate as well as individual. Wesley's General Rules required that early Methodists attend church services where the Bible was taught and preached. In addition,

Wesleyan hymns, heavily based on Scripture, were another part of the corporate discipline of encountering God through the Bible.[16]

Reflect

What is your experience of reading and studying the Bible? What benefits do you see in this practice? How might it be challenging?

Fasting

Wesley believed fasting to be an important means of staying in love with God. Although he thought that fasting had sometimes been used in extreme ways, he advocated a balanced approach to this discipline. He recommended fasting for one day from food, but not from water. For him the benefits of fasting were to bring persons into a temperate way of living and to provide more time for prayer and encountering God.[17] Wesley himself mainly followed the Anglican practice of fasting on Fridays and during the forty days of Lent. During some periods of his life, he followed and encouraged the practice of abstinence rather than total fasting. That is, he refrained from certain foods. Wesley disapproved of the ascetic use of fasting for bodily mortification, a historic practice in part of the Christian tradition. Instead, fasting was to be used as a means of grace, a way of receiving the gifts of God.[18]

Reflect

What is your response to Wesley's ideas about fasting as a spiritual discipline? How might it be challenging for you? How might it be beneficial?

WHAT DOES THE BIBLE SAY?

The Bible offers important insights into the practice of spiritual disciplines that help us to stay in love with God.

Read the following Bible passages. What challenges you or makes you want to know more in the readings? What do they say to you about ways to stay in love with God?

Dcutcronomy 6:4-9

Matthew 22:34-40

1 Kings 8

John 4

Reflect on the Bible

Deuteronomy 6:4-9

The Book of Deuteronomy is presented as an oration by Moses in the plains of Moab at the end of the wilderness wanderings. Directed to the people of Israel before they cross the Jordan into Canaan, this book is a call to remember their slavery in Egypt, God's deliverance in the Exodus, and the covenant at Horeb. Deuteronomy 6:4-9 is called the Shema, the

Hebrew word for *hear*. This passage is a fundamental commandment about how Israel is to be faithful. The people of Israel are to give complete obedience to the *one* God. As covenant people they are to love God with all their heart, soul, and might. In Hebrew, the word for *heart* is much broader in meaning than it is for us today. *Heart* means the combination of what we would call intellect, will, and soul, indeed the wholeness of the person. The faithful are to teach this command to their children in answer to their questions so that generation after generation will remember God.

Reflect

What do you love with all your heart, soul, and might? What connections do you see between this love and your love for God?

Matthew 22:34-40

In first-century rabbinical discussions, a common question was which of the more than six hundred commandments of the Law was the most important. That is the background of this question to Jesus. Here Jesus answers that question with the Shema and combines it with Leviticus 19:18, "You shall love your neighbor as yourself." In this chapter, we are considering practices that keep us in love with God. Jesus places love for God alongside love for neighbor. Love for God is illustrated in love for one's neighbor. We can say that Jesus offers the commandment to stay in love with God and a practice for doing so. Love for neighbor is a witness to and a remembering of one's love for God, a love that empowers all other loves.

Reflect

What connections do you see between love for God and love for neighbor?

1 Kings 8

In 1 Kings 8 we find the story of Solomon's dedication of the great Temple in Jerusalem, the dwelling place of God in the midst of the Hebrew people and a place giving them identity. This is where they will worship, feast, and receive instruction in the Torah. Solomon consecrates the Temple with a prayer renewing Israel's covenant with God. In this prayer he asks a rhetorical question and then answers it: "But will God indeed dwell on the earth? Even heaven and the highest heaven cannot contain you, much less the house that I have built!" (verse 27). God cannot be contained, yet the Temple is an important reminder of Israel's call to worship God. Another way this story affirms God's presence in the world beyond the Temple, and indeed beyond Israel, is Solomon's call for God to hear the prayers of both Israel and Gentiles offered from this Temple (verses 28-30, 41-43). The prayer petition affirms that God's love for humanity is not limited to Israel but is inclusive of all peoples.

How does worship at your church help you stay in love with God?

Reflect

John 4

The story of Jesus' encounter with the Samaritan woman is familiar. We know of the uniqueness of this encounter between a Jewish man and a Samaritan woman. We remember their conversation about living water. And we recall Jesus' knowing about her five former husbands and current lover. Jesus is the one who reveals who she really is. However, the story places an important focus on the practice of worship as a way of encountering God. Well into the conversation the woman declares Jesus to be a prophet, and that declaration turns their focus to worship. The setting is important. Near a Samaritan holy place she is talking with one she believes to be a Jewish prophet. With this understanding she raises an indirect question about the correct place to worship: "Our ancestors worshiped on this mountain, but you say that the place where people must worship is in Jerusalem" (verse 20). She uses the term "our ancestors" because Jews and Samaritans have some of the same ancestry. "This mountain" refers to Mount Gerizim, where there had been a Samaritan temple. Jesus answers, "Woman, believe me, the hour is coming when you will worship the Father neither on this mountain nor in Jerusalem" (verse 21).

Gail O'Day makes the point that Jesus indicates who is being worshiped—the Father. Jesus announces that "the hour is coming, and is now here, when true worshipers will worship the Father in spirit and in truth, for the Father seeks such as these to worship him" (John 4:23). O'Day says his statement points to a true and full worship of God that reflects knowledge of who God is. We become true worshipers of God through recognizing Jesus' identity and being in relationship with him.[19] Worship is more about one's spirit and the truth of God's power and presence than it is about locations. It's not about temples and mountains alone, but about turning one's heart to God.

Reflect

Is your experience of God's presence different in corporate worship than in other settings? If so, why? What connections do you see in the location of worship and the attitude of worship?

CLOSING – A GUIDE FOR DAILY PRAYER

Welcoming God's Presence

Loving God, we seek to love you with all our heart, soul, and might. Make your presence known to us and guide us in our longings. In Christ's name. Amen.

Scripture

"As a deer longs for flowing streams,
   so my soul longs for you, O God.
My soul thirsts for God,
   for the living God.

When shall I come and behold
   the face of God?"
                    — Psalm 42:1-2

Meditation

Reflect on these verses from Psalm 42. What have you longed for? What do your longings tell you about your longing for God? What spiritual practices have led you closer to God?

Prayer

Pray for discernment about the place of these practices in your faith journey.

Blessing

"Prayer may be said to be the breath of our spiritual life."
             — John Wesley, *Explanatory Notes: 1 Thess. 5:16*[20]

---

[1] *The Book of Discipline*, "The Nature, Design, and General Rules of Our United Societies," ¶ 103 (The United Methodist Publishing House, 2004); p. 74.

[2] Joerg Rieger, "The Means of Grace, John Wesley, and the Theological Dilemma of the Church Today," *Quarterly Review* (Winter 1997–98); p. 380. See also *John Wesley's Theology: A Collection From His Works*, edited by Robert W. Burtner and Robert E. Chiles (Abingdon, 1982); pp. 229–230.

[3] Steve Harper, *Devotional Life in the Wesleyan Tradition* (The Upper Room, 1983); p. 19.

[4] Quoted in Harper; p. 19.

[5] Harper; pp. 20–23, 75.

[6] Harper; p. 24.

[7] Hoyt Hickman, *Worshiping With United Methodists* (Abingdon, 1996); p. 46.

[8] Albert Outler, ed., *John Wesley* (Oxford University Press, 1964); p. 332.

[9] Quoted in W. Stephen Gunter, ed., *The Quotable Mr. Wesley* (Candler School of Theology, 2003); p. 57.

[10] Hickman; p. 47

[11] Harper; pp. 37–38.

[12] Outler; p. 333.

[13] Harper; p. 38.

[14] Harper; pp. 28–29.

[15] Harper; pp. 30–32.

[16] Harper; pp. 33–34.
[17] Harper; pp. 47–49.
[18] Harper; pp. 50–52.
[19] Gail O'Day, *Revelation in the Fourth Gospel* (Fortress, 1986); pp. 68–71.
[20] Quoted in Gunter; p. 36.

Chapter

Stay in Love With God — Practicing the Rule

Focus Question:

How can we put into practice the rule of staying in love with God? What difference can our practice make in our own lives and in the lives of others?

A Prayer

O God of unlimited love, help us in all the demands and challenges of our daily lives to choose and put into action one or more practices that will enable us to stay in love with you.

WHAT DOES THE RULE SAY?

The third of Wesley's three rules is, in Rueben Job's words, "stay in love with God." The spiritual disciplines help us to show up and pay attention to our relationship to God, to learn of God's love for us, and to learn to love what God loves. The main traditional practices are prayer, worship and the Lord's Supper, reading and studying the Bible, and fasting. However, as Job writes, "We may name our spiritual disciplines differently, but we too must find our way of living and practicing those disciplines that will keep us in love with God" (*Three Simple Rules*; p. 55).

Reflect on the Rule

What are your initial ideas about what it means to practice staying in love with God? What has been your experience and understanding of the role of spiritual disciplines in your life? What role do each of the following spiritual disciplines play in your life? Which means most to you? Why?

Prayer

Worship and the Lord's Supper

Reading and studying the Bible

Fasting

The Upper Decks

Writer Doris Donnelly tells the story of her great-aunt's voyage to America. Donnelly's grandmother hadn't seen her sister, Greta, who lived in

Holland, for twenty-five years. When she sent money for Greta to immigrate, Greta immediately booked passage on the first steamer out of Rotterdam. Instead of waiting six months for better accommodations, she settled for steerage. On the ship was a purser who regularly invited families traveling in the crowded uncomfortable conditions in the lower deck to come to the upper decks during the day. When the purser invited Greta, she refused the offer and spent the two-week voyage on her bunk in the hold of the ship.

When the ship docked in New York, Greta finally came out of steerage to the upper decks and she was amazed at what she saw. There were comfortable, well-appointed areas where travelers could socialize, feast, and enjoy their leisure. More surprising to Greta was the sight of other passengers from steerage who had accepted the invitation. All this could have been hers, too, had she only shown up to receive the gift. Donnelly told Greta's story in the context of an essay on the spiritual life. She said that many people think the spiritual life is for other people, more advanced in faith and discipleship. They don't realize that the spiritual life is for everyone. It is available for the taking.[1] It is about showing up and paying attention, and the way to do that is through spiritual disciplines or practices.

> What connections do you make with Greta's story? What does this story say to you about God's grace? About practices that will help you to stay in love with God?
>
> **Reflect**

Prayer

In his letter to the Romans, Paul writes we do not know how to pray as we ought (Romans 8:26). Many Christians would agree, but there's nothing wrong with being an amateur at prayer. People pray many different ways—with words and with silence, with others and alone. Some like to have prayer books or devotional guides to prompt them. Some people draw their prayers. Others pray through their music. Brother Lawrence prayed as he washed dishes. One person I know prays as she swims laps. Prayer is connecting with God. Traditional forms are praise, thanksgiving, confession, petition, and intercession. Some liturgical prayers attempt to include all these forms. Most private prayers are just a couple of these. Journaling is a discipline that can be prayer. Granted, journal writing can be self-serving and self-absorbing. Whether or not journaling is a prayer discipline depends largely on what we bring to it. Are we trying to be honest about ourselves before God? As we write, are we engaging with our other practices of faith—reading Scripture, connecting with the worshiping community, and works of love and justice? Are we listening for what God is saying to us?

Reflect

> How has your concept of prayer changed throughout your journey of faith? What experiences have prompted you to practice different forms of prayer?

Worship and the Lord's Supper

Regular attendance at worship nurtures us in the Christian life. Through liturgy, Scripture readings, sermons, and hymns we are formed in the Christian tradition and connected to the entire Christian world as well as to a particular community of Christians. We join them in praising God. Our worship reminds us of who God is and helps us remember that our first allegiance is to God, not to the people, systems, and things that we are tempted to worship instead of the God of all creation.

Central to worship is the Lord's Supper. In this meal God offers God's own being and love, and in this meal we remember what God in Christ has done for us. As Paul writes, "The cup of blessing that we bless, is it not a sharing in the blood of Christ? The bread that we break, is it not a sharing in the body of Christ?" (1 Corinthians 10:16). Then we are sent out to be the body of Christ in the world. Indeed, we are able to love our neighbors because "Christ first loved us." When we read Paul's account of the words of institution, we are reading about the meal that the Christian community was already celebrating. It gave them their identity and shaped their ministry. As they had received, they were able to give. Literally a re-membering or "putting together again," in this meal the scattered members of the body came together and were empowered by their worship to be in ministry in the world beyond their gathering.

Being a part of a worshiping community keeps us connected to God in ways that go beyond Sunday morning worship. In this community we learn more about living out the Christian faith and we are empowered to do works of justice and mercy in the world.

> How does attending and participating in worship and the Lord's Supper help you experience God's power and presence? How do these practices affect your daily life? How might they affect your life in the future?
>
> **Reflect**

Reading and Studying Scripture

Meditation on Scripture, also called *lectio divina* (literally, holy reading), is a discipline that causes us to pay attention to the words, slowly and reflectively. Writer Kathleen Norris describes her experience of *lectio divina* in *The Cloister Walk*. Her regular participation in morning or evening prayer with monks in a Benedictine monastery led her to remark, "I find it a blessing that monks still respect the slow way that words work on the human psyche."[2]

We can also participate in this kind of spiritual reading in private by pondering a passage of Scripture and listening for what the Spirit has to say to us through it. Journaling, as you are doing in this study, can be a part of *lectio divina*. Reading Scripture as a spiritual discipline is different from the kind of Bible study in which we learn information—the historical context of a passage, the ways it has been interpreted, and its connections with other passages of Scripture. Learning about Scripture is, of course, an essential aspect of discipleship; but spiritual reading is more about nurturing our relationship with God than about acquiring information. In whatever way you engage the Bible, though, whether to gain information or to seek relationship with God, God speaks and transforms us through the encounter. What is important is to open it, read it, and let God speak to you.

How often do you read the Bible? Do you read to gain information or to nurture relationship with God? Which way of reading speaks most to you or nurtures you? Why?

Fasting

Although fasting has been a central spiritual discipline in Hebrew and Christian traditions, it has been on the periphery for many Protestants. A vestige of fasting is found in our practice of giving something up for Lent—something like chocolate, dessert, sodas, or caffeine. Spiritual writer Marjorie Thompson calls this token observance "the trivialization of a very profound discipline."[3] Thompson points out that for the early church, Lent was not about restriction and self-torture. Instead, it was opportunity to recognize our human limits and idolatries so that we make God the center of our lives. Fasting is a practice that helps us to connect with God because it enables us to see what is ultimately important.

Traditionally, fasting has meant giving up food, but not water, for a certain period of time—for example, from noon until noon the next day. Health issues must be taken into account when one considers fasting that involves food. However, there are other forms of fasting. In our materialistic society of overindulgence, we could choose to give up things that distract us and take our attention away from God. We might give up watching TV, shopping for things we don't need, or our desire for achievement and recognition.

What comes to your mind when you consider the practice of fasting? What challenges you about this practice? What benefits do you see in this practice? Do you think that some form of fasting might help you stay in love with God? Why or why not?

WHAT DOES THE BIBLE SAY?

The Bible offers helpful perspectives that can help us as we reflect on spiritual practices that will help us to stay in love with God.

Read the following Scriptures. How do they speak to you about the spiritual disciplines of prayer, worship and the Lord's Supper, reading and studying the Bible, and fasting? What do they suggest to you about the importance of spiritual disciplines as a way of staying in love with God?

Daniel 1 and 6

Luke 11:1-13

1 Corinthians 11:23-26

Reflect on the Bible

Daniel 1 and 6

The Book of Daniel is an encouragement to Jews who were in exile. Daniel and his friends are role models who remain faithful to Jewish law and the faith of Israel even though they serve a foreign king. Daniel is a Jewish exile in Babylon who is admired in the king's court for his wisdom and ability to interpret dreams. In Daniel 1, when Daniel was expected to eat the royal rations of food and wine, he asked that he be allowed to keep the dietary laws of his people. Eating certain kinds of food were an important part of his spiritual discipline. Daniel 6 tells about a plot in which Daniel was expected to pray to King Nebuchadnezzar. Daniel, however, continues to pray to God. The king has to throw him into the lion's den. However, the king hopes that Daniel will survive; and sure enough, the next morning the king finds Daniel still alive. The king then issues an edict that the Babylonian people will worship Daniel's God. Both these chapters point to the importance of spiritual disciplines in Daniel's relationship with God.

Reflect

How does Daniel's example affect you as you consider your practice of spiritual disciplines? How has a spiritual discipline served to ground you and hold you steadfast during a difficult time?

Luke 11:1-13

The disciples ask Jesus to teach them how to pray, and the prayer he teaches is the one we know and love as the Lord's Prayer. At those times when we feel we simply don't have words to pray, this is a good place to start. Even when the words of a prayer come readily to our lips, this prayer is a pattern we can use. It is a prayer of blessing, confession and forgiveness, petition, and intercession for the world. It begins with acknowledging God's holiness and asking for God's kingdom, that is, God's realm of justice, compassion, and mercy. It asks for what we need to sustain us. As it requests forgiveness, it recognizes the need to forgive one another. The two are interdependent in this prayer. Finally, it requests God's salvation during times of temptation, trial, or evil. This prayer contains within itself the recognition of what is needed to nurture faithfulness in individuals and in communities.

Reflect

Examine the Lord's Prayer as a pattern for your own prayers. How can you learn to pray by using it as a pattern? In what new ways can it speak to you about God's presence and power and your life of faith? How do you think this prayer can help you stay in love with God?

1 Corinthians 11:23-26

In 1 Corinthians 11:17-22, Paul writes that he does not approve of the way the Corinthians conduct their life together. There are divisions and factions that do not serve the community. Some Corinthians turn the Lord's Supper into an individual exercise of piety, resulting in drunkenness on the part of some and hunger on the part of others. Paul tells them that they are showing contempt for the church and humiliating those who are poor. To correct their abuses, Paul reminds them of the tradition. In verse 23 when he says, "For I received from the Lord what I also handed on to you," he is using words that denote receiving and handing on a tradition. In this case, the tradition goes back to Jesus who instituted the Supper on the night he was betrayed. That reminder shows the contrast between the seriousness of the occasion and the party the Corinthians made of it. As traditionally happened in Jewish meals, Jesus took bread, gave thanks, and broke it. This act represented the offering of the life of Jesus for those who follow in his way. Paul told them that the supper was to be repeated "in remembrance" of Christ. This word *remembrance* means more than recalling an event. Rather, it means to make the event present. When Paul says, "As often as you eat this bread and drink the cup, you proclaim the Lord's death until he comes," he is regarding the Lord's Supper as proclamation of God's redeeming act in Christ, which is not only a past event but also a present and future event (verse 26). The unity that Paul is encouraging the Corinthians to observe would be an expression of their loving and caring for each other. They are to regard and respect each other as equals.

What do Paul's words about the significance of the Lord's Supper say to you about the practice of staying in love with God by sharing the Lord's Supper with others? How do you think this practice offers nurture and power for living as a follower of Jesus Christ? How do you think this practice contributes to the unity of the Christian community?

Reflect

Conclusion

As you come to the close of this study, my prayer is that you will find the particular disciplines that will help you stay in close relationship with God and empower you to live out God's call for your life of faithful discipleship. The three simple rules will hold great power for you as you seek to live the way of Christ. First, do no harm. Do good. And stay in love with God.

Reflect

After considering the three simple rules, which one seems the most challenging for you at this time of your life? What choices or changes can you make in order to live out the three simple rules for Christian living?

CLOSING – A GUIDE FOR DAILY PRAYER

Welcoming God's Presence

O God, awaken us to your presence and help us to attend to the practices that keep us in love with you. Keep us mindful of the ways these practices keep us in love with you and with our sisters and brothers as we strive to do no harm and to do good. Amen.

Scripture

I wait for the LORD, my soul waits,
  and in his word I hope;
my soul waits for the Lord
   more than those who watch for the morning,
   more than those who watch for the morning.
                    — Psalm 130:5-6

Meditation

Ponder the ways you wait for God and enjoy God's companionship.

Prayer

Pray for the resolve to show up for the practices of faith and pay attention to the workings of the Spirit in your life.

Blessing

"Rejoice always, pray without ceasing, give thanks in all circumstances; for this is the will of God in Christ Jesus for you."
— 1 Thessalonians 5:16-18

---

[1] Doris Donnelly, "Is the Spiritual Life for Everyone?" *Weavings*, Vol. 1, No. 1 (September/October 1986); pp. 6–7.

[2] Kathleen Norris, *The Cloister Walk* (Riverhead Books, 1996); p. 145.

[3] Marjorie J. Thompson, *Soul Feast* (Westminster John Knox, 1995); p. 72.